Pearl's Diary

Eben May

Published by K.A.Edwards, 2024.

PEARL'S DIARY

First edition. April 2, 2024.

ISBN: 979-8224355730

Written by Eben May.

Table of Contents

To Mama and Papa Stadem With Love

Although the main character in this book is Pearl Stadem, the author Eben May, her son, has fondly shared his mother's memories, in the form of stories about her life on the Prairie farm.

It all began in the early 1900s in South Dakota, when life was simple, adaptable and yet enjoyable. Eben May hopes others will enjoy these stories, as much as all the grandchildren and great-grandchildren who first heard them.

Pearl Stadem shared these wonderful stories, at joyous family reunions at the farm every year. These simple, yet humble stories embody Pearl's golden memories of loved ones and a tidy, Scandinavian pioneer family home.

The scene is set on a farm which was eighty-eight acres, on the mighty buffalo's former range. America was rapidly changing, even then with the arrival of railroads. But some things need not change, since they remain enshrined in hearts of those who lived in those nation-building times.

In Pearl's home, love and regard for others grew strong and steadfast. Standing tall like the rippling waves of flowered Prairie grass, that once stretched unfenced, to every horizon and far beyond.

Her diary is a doorway into the truly challenging and exciting life of pioneers that can, through her sharp eyes and daily experiences, open possibilities of blessing, humor, surprise, renewal, and discovery for all of us.

• • • •

Eben May,
Wingshadow Lodge,
Washington State

My Very First Diary

Dear Diary: Today Mama bought me my very first diary book. I was so excited, I couldn't wait to write in it. What shall I write about? I know, I will begin with my name!

My name is Pearl Stadem and I have six sisters, Bernice, Myrtle, Cora, Alita, Estelle, and Ruth. We live with our Mama and Papa on a farm.

Our farm is the biggest farm in the world, well, maybe not in the world, but it is very, very, very, very big.

We have many different animals on our farm, like dogs and barn cats, (barn cats are my favorite animals). There are cows, sheep, horses, chickens, all kinds of bird-life like pheasants, and even deer!

Papa works very hard on the farm, and sometimes I help him with his work. Mama said that I am a big girl now, big enough to help on the farm. I help Papa milk the cows, collect the eggs from the chicken coop and feed all of the animals.

I love my farm. It is so beautiful here.

I go to school everyday, except Saturday and Sunday. Sometimes I walk or sometimes I ride a horse.

On Sundays, we all go to Church four miles away in a town called Bryant.

When Papa and Mama and my sisters moved to our new farm, it was not as beautiful. We all worked hard to move all the rocks from the fields, to make it beautiful. Papa used all these rocks to make foundations for barns and other buildings. Now the farm is beautiful. I love my farm!

* * * *

PEARL'S WISDOM: EVERY farm needs a big girl like me, to help make it beautiful!

Many Hands Make Light Work!

Dear Diary: Papa was wonderful how he taught us to work on the farm. He showed each of us girls how to handle loads. Just by watching our feet, and where we stepped, taught us not to trip and get hurt.

Carrying a bucket of milk was one of those things we had to do right, or lose it all on the ground.

I learned from him how to harness the horses, and even how to hitch up the buggy.

Plowing was the hardest thing of all. He taught me how to handle the horses, to pull the plow straight across a field. I did that at the age of eight, imagine that!

Plowing was tricky, because you had to keep going. You had to keep your eyes ahead fixed on some landmark, or your furrow would wander. Then the field would soon be a mess of missed patches of grass.

Good thing I was born far-sighted! I had to look across the unplowed field to a tiny spot, acres away, and kept the team of horses and the plow headed straight at it!

Papa made work easier for us whenever he could. We had to clear the fields of rocks, after it was plowed. He hitched a big plank behind a horse. We could push stones over on it, and not have to lift the heavy rocks up to a wagon. Then he hauled the rocks to wherever he had a pile.

Why did Papa save the rocks? He needed them to use with cement, to make foundations for our new house we were building.

I had by that time learned how to tend the stock, lead cows to water and pasture, plow, take care of chickens, and milk cows, you name it.

I was Papa's eldest child and daughter, and I was doing a boy's work. But Papa didn't mind, neither did I.

On other farms with boys, I would be kept in the house only to learn how to cook, clean the house, bed-making, laundry, quilt-making, etc.

But I learned not only those things, I also learned men's outdoor work too!

Good thing my six sisters came along to help me. I would never been able to keep it up as I did without them.

Many hands make light work, they say. Well, not exactly. But I can say my six sisters made my chores lighter, until Brother Art finally came along. By that time, I was doing a man's work!

I cared for Art when he was a baby too, and our first baby brother was worth it! We girls adored him, but somehow it never seemed to spoil him, ever.

• • • •

PEARL'S WISDOM: LIVING on a farm can be hard work, especially without brothers. If you can, get a baby brother or two or three, their hands will certainly make your farm work light!

Dear Diary: Papa was born and raised in a sod-house. That was what pioneers were made to dwell in, before houses could be built.

It was one or two rooms, dug out of the ground. It was a kind of basement dwelling, with walls extending up above the surface, built up of bricks of grass sod cut in squares.

To keep the walls stable, a couple of windows were put in on the sides. They weren't big and didn't shed much light. Glass was expensive too, so windows were almost a luxury in a "soddie," as we called it.

Our great grandfather had built his sod house, for our Papa when he was little, his little brother, a sister, and their mother to live in it. The only thing was it was dark, and not so healthy to live that way.

As soon as the pioneers could, they bought lumber and built houses with windows, so they could move out of the dugouts.

Moving near to the old dugout where Papa had lived, we children got to go there sometimes, to see it and played pioneer in it.

The wood stove was gone, bed and furnishings were gone too. We found some old crates and a broken chair to play with. We also found a few other things such as a cup, and two cracked plates to use. We played house, just as we imagined they did it, when Papa lived there. We too were real pioneers, we thought.

Corn grew right around the dugout, so it was hard to find the dugout when the corn was growing.

The old path to it never sprouted corn, even when plowed under. Maybe because deer and other animals used it from old habits, and kept the corn sprouts from growing.

You had to look out where you were running though, as you might even meet a snake, big or small. It would sun itself on the path, or lay hidden in the thick, high, prairie grass that grew on unplowed fields.

One time, I was running through tall grass across the road from our farm, in my bare feet. I suddenly felt something soft and squishy underfoot. I knew it had to be a bull snake, a big one too!

How I howled and jumped! I kept on running home to be safe, although I knew bull snakes caught gophers and mice, and weren't poisonous.

Scary, yes, but that was part of the ordinary life on the Prairie. Wild creatures did not know they were on our farm. They had always lived there after all.

Even if some of the wild creatures scared me sometimes, I knew they were our neighbors. I soon calmed myself down and went back to doing chores, that helped keep the family farm running smoothly.

• • • •

PEARL'S WISDOM: WILD creatures share our world too, and most all of them help to make it a better place. But don't ever step on a bull snake, it is scary how squishy they are!

Dear Diary: My little sisters, the baby and I were on our grandparents' farm. We were three miles away from the new farm Papa bought.

We came home from school and found Papa and Mama gone. But we knew where they would be. They were preparing the new farm so we could move there.

Rather than to sit and wait for them to return, I had a bright idea.

I had often watched Papa hitch up the horse to the buggy. He fixed the harness securely on the horse, and attached the buggy's hitch. I felt sure I could do it.

My sisters were excited as they watched me harness the horse, then make a go at the hitch.

When I got all that done, we were ready to start off for our new place.

I knew the way, having gone with Papa and Mama many times already. We moved things, large and small in a big wagon.

The wind felt good on our faces as we were very excited.

"Whoa!" I cried to our trusty horse, when we arrived at the new farm.

Papa and Mama looked us over and didn't say anything as we pulled up. I stood shifting my feet about, wondering why they weren't pleased to see us.

Papa went and looked at how the hitch was done. Then he showed me it was partly on, and partly off.

Oh, no! The hitch might have come loose, if we had hit a bump or rock in the road. What then? With the buggy separated from the horse, we might have crashed and all gone flying out, that's what?

Feeling uneasy, I waited for the word of correction and some kind of punishment. But, no, nothing of the sort was given to me.

I was so surprised and relieved I didn't get punished.

Papa knew what he showed me was enough, to let me know how it could have all gone very wrong. My risky adventure with the horse, buggy, my sisters and the baby, came out all right, thankfully.

It is so important to hitch the horse and buggy right, or it will wreck the buggy, or worse, it can cause a lot of hurt.

• • • •

PEARL'S WISDOM: IT may seem like fun to do grown-up things, but if not done right can cause a world of hurt!

A Home of Our Very Own!

Dear Diary: Papa saved up enough money to buy eighty-eight acres of land. He moved our family near to it, in order to have our own farm.

Until then we lived and worked on a farm, belonging to the pastor of our church in town. Now at last we could have our own home to keep! We were all excited beyond words!

The land Papa bought had belonged to his uncle. He may have sold it to him for less than it's worth. That was the loving way families and relatives helped each other in those early days. Otherwise, who could have made it on the Prairie as pioneers? Few, indeed!

Filling the wagon with our belongings, pulled by our horse and mule, we set off to our new home. The only problem was where would we live on it?

Papa had thought it out carefully. A medium-sized shed stood on the property, along with a barn, an outhouse, a hen house and some fencing for stock.

Papa had the shed fixed with a small wood stove, a crib for the baby, and some mattresses for us to sleep on. Our clothes would go in boxes. They were stacked one on top the other, to keep them off the dirt floor.

The shed scarcely had enough room for us all, with more children to come, but we squeezed in anyway.

How wonderful, despite the cramped shed, to live and work on our own land!

It was lovely, despite mud, dust, chores, biting insects, freezing cold winter winds, and scorching hot temperatures in the summer.

Home Sweet Home! Why? Because it was ours! We slept in the shed the first night we moved. I dreamed of all the things we were going to do, to help Papa make it the best and the happiest farm in the world.

The first big project, now that we had moved, was to build a frame for our house.

With much hard work, our beautiful home will be completed. Then we can begin work on the farm!

• • • •

PEARL'S WISDOM: THERE is nothing like home sweet home, especially when you helped to build it!

How I Stopped a Runaway Windmill!

Dear Diary: One day it was very windy on the farm. I saw that the windmill was spinning so fast that it wasn't going to last at that rate. It didn't sound right either, and was maybe broken already.

I had to do something, but what? We needed the windmill. It could be ruined by the strong wind, that was making it run out of control like that.

Mama didn't know what to do, but I did. Mama was taking care of my baby sister, so it was up to me to do something.

"I can fix it," I thought. This was dangerous man's work, not a big girl's normally. Papa had gone to town, so now it was a big girl's job!

"I'll be praying for you!" said Mama. And she prayed!

I climbed up the windmill. When I got to the spot, where the moving parts were, leading to the whirling blades, I saw just what I needed to do.

I could have been hurt, but Mama's prayers lifted me up. I pushed the wooden part going up and down that drew the water up. It rammed against the frame, and the windmill's whirling blades stopped!

When I got back to the ground, Mama looked at me amazed, that I could do such a thing, to save the windmill.

But really and truly, she knew big girls can do amazing things, sometimes!

. . . .

PEARL'S WISDOM: A GIRL can be strong enough, to fix a runaway windmill, especially when her Mama prays!

Dear Diary: We had a dog called Sandy on the farm, but she needed another dog to be friends with. So, I told Papa that we should get that special friend for Sandy. Papa agreed.

One day, a friend of Papa, named Uncle Jack, came to visit us at the farm, and he brought his dog with him. Uncle Jack lived in Denver, Colorado, and he called his dog Denver, after the city he lived in.

Denver was a young white and brown spotted, mix-breed dog. Immediately, he took to Sandy and they played rather nicely together. But when Uncle Jack was ready to leave, Denver wanted to stay with his new best friend Sandy.

Uncle Jack decided to give us his dog Denver. Besides, he would have a lot more room to run around on the farm. Plus, he had Sandy, his new best friend.

Papa accepted Denver the dog at once, as he had planned to get another dog for the farm.

Denver was the friendliest and the most lovable dog you could ever want. He never caused us any trouble by running off at all. This showed that he took to Papa right off, and didn't want to leave him, and of course his new friend Sandy.

Denver the dog loves living on the farm, and took to farm life, as if he had always lived there.

He loves running around and having a good time with Sandy.

On the farm, he will have plenty of space, clean air, and no cars or trucks to dodge, unlike living in the city.

Now Sandy will never be lonely again.

· · · ·

PEARL'S WISDOM: EVEN dogs get lonely and would welcome a pal, especially on a farm!

Dear Diary: Our farm sloped down to a low place. There, water collected from the rain and snow to form a pond.

The grass grew up high in it in the spring time. The water would stay most of the summer, so it really came in handy.

Papa showed me how to drive the horse and wagon down in the water, just far enough to get the wheels wet. That helped the wood to swell, and kept the iron rims from slipping off.

Our horses, cattle, and sheep, just like the buffalo before them, loved the slough in spring and summer time. They went down to graze in the lush grass growing out of it. They also liked to stand in it in the deep end, as they used it to cool off.

No doubt their hooves sank to the bottom of the mud, which was even cooler than the water.

Have you ever put your bare feet into cool mud on a hot day? Wriggled your toes in it? It is a wonderful feeling.

Mama's garden of flowers and vegetables, depended on this water too. To water it, we hitched a big plank to a horse, put a big barrel on it, then the horse dragged it down to the slough.

It was a bumpy ride! Soon we were able to fill the barrel using buckets.

When it was full, we started back hoping for the best.

This was the hardest part. The tipsy barrel didn't take too well to the bumps, and the water sloshed out.

By the time we got the barrel up to the yard, half the precious water was lost. Even though my sisters held on to the barrel as best they could.

We also used the slough to swim in to cool off. It was too grassy to really swim, and not very deep, but we pretended it was and had fun thinking it was our own little lake.

In the winter things changed with the freezing cold. The water was very low by that time usually. If enough rain fell in the fall, there might be some stretches of ice to play on.

Snow covered it too, but we could clear it off with a shovel. Our skates? Papa's skates were too big, but we could slide in our boots at least.

The old slough, as we all called it, was used by many wild creatures besides us. Birds drank from it. Frogs lived in it. Thirsty deer came for a drink. I often saw the run off when I came.

A raccoon, now and then, visited. Coyotes and foxes no doubt. But what I would have loved to see, were the buffalos and their calves that once spent part of every summer here, feeding on the lush grass.

The slough is great for many uses, and some of them were even fun!

• • • •

PEARL'S WISDOM: THE best things in life are free. Nobody on farms like ours ever paid for water, and our Rainmaker didn't charge us a penny!

Mama and the Can of Cream

Dear Diary: Our cows had done very well this past week, making the can in the cistern full to the brim!

Mama had made out a list of things she wanted to buy in exchange for our cream, butter, and eggs that we were going to sell.

I harnessed up the horse and hitched the buggy, then I drove it to the back porch.

Papa loaded the can of cream into the buggy, while Mama, Bernice, and Estelle piled in. My other sisters had to stay home to keep things going until we returned.

We were riding along just fine and merrily, when something made a big noise in back. The sound came from the back of the buggy, where Papa had set the cream can, eggs, and butter.

When I stopped the buggy, we tried to figure out what was wrong.

We all looked over our seat into the back compartment. Something was missing. Oh, no! The cream can, it was gone!

I jumped down and went around the back, with my two sisters. We stare with horror at the white trail of cream. Then we saw the can itself which lay in the ditch, with the cover off and cream gushing out.

I called out to Mama, who was still sitting in the buggy, that the cream can had fallen out, and all the cream lost in the ditch.

Mama came to take a look and told us not to worry. She said that we can scoop it all back in the can, as it was laying only on the grass.

Mama then knelt down and started scooping, using the can cover.

I knew we had something better, so I ran to the buggy to fetch a big grain scoop. I gave it to Mama, which made it easier for her to continue scooping up the cream.

The five gallons didn't soak into the ground, as it was lying on top the thick mat of grass.

Thanks to the grass, she got most all of it back into the can.

Our hands were very sticky, and Mama had some spots of cream on her dress where she knelt down.

We carried the heavy can back to the rear of the buggy, then we continued on to town.

I parked in front the Bryant granary and mill store, where I tied the horse to the hitching post.

We could sell our goods there, where they would be taken by the railway company, to some big city along the railway line.

A big boy came out of the store and took our goods inside for us.

Mr. Tomasson was at the big desk counter that stood higher than us. He got the boy to take the can of cream, to weigh it on a big company weighing scale.

Mama went to Mr. Tomasson with a look of concern on her face.

She told him, that the can of cream fell over in the ditch, but we had scooped the cream back into the can. She asked him if he would still take it this way?

Mr. Tomasson just laughed and said that it was okay, that sometimes worse than that happened to the goods he bought.

Mama was relieved and so were we. Saturday's sale worked out good after all!

Next, the General Store to sell the butter and eggs, then finally to shop for Mama's list of groceries.

• • • •

PEARL'S WISDOM: CRYING over spilt cream was no good, no more than crying over spilt milk. If possible scoop it back up, and save your tears!

Dear Diary: Papa was a special kind of man, for he was a well-digging expert in the community. He earned a little money for the family this way on the side, other than his farming and auctioneering.

Papa knew his business too! He wouldn't go into a hole, until he had determined it was safe for him. To see if it was safe, he had a rooster or an old hen who stopped laying eggs, or pecked other hens brought by me. It was then let down into the deep hole.

The next day, if the rooster was okay, Papa knew it was safe for a man too!

Papa could find water, which was the reason for the wells, after all. That was a valuable gift of his.

He found water for many people on their farms. He could tell somehow where it was running beneath the ground.

This was not something everybody could do. Imagine, digging a deep hole and you got nothing but dirt for all that hard work!

Farmers wanted to know where there was going to be water, before they dug such deep holes! So, they hired Papa, who was almost certain to find water for them!

Now why was a rooster put down in the hole when it was dug out? The reason was simple. Gas out of the newly dug earth could seep into the hole, and it was strong enough to make you sick, or even kill you.

Coal miners, I learned in school, took a canary down into a deep mine for the same reason. The gas could even catch afire and explode, if it came next to the fire of a lantern or match.

You can imagine, how important it was to check for gas in the job of well-digging. You never knew, unless you checked, where there might be gas in the ground.

So, with the possibility of the hole caving in, and the dangerous gas, well-digging was not something Papa took lightly. He knew just how to handle it, however, and never had an accident.

As for the poor old rooster, I felt sorry for it having to go down into that deep dark well. I was so glad when, the next day, it was brought out safe and sound!

• • • •

PEARL'S WISDOM: IF you don't have a canary to be a gas-alarm in a well, a rooster will definitely work!

How I Got Home in the Dark

Dear Diary: Papa told me to take the horse and buggy home from town, knowing that he would get a ride back to the farm later.

He had to go to a very important meeting there in town. But, he told me to go home alone, when it was getting dark! I guess he felt he could trust me.

I had two horses hitched to the buggy. It was getting so dark, and I was a little bit concerned. How was I to find my way without light? But, I knew the horses knew the way.

So, I let the reins drop and the horses kept moving in the dark. I wasn't even afraid one bit!

Sure enough, the horses knew just where to turn, from one road to the next. I sang a little song to show how brave I was!

Soon, after several miles, and many verses of Lou, Lou, Skip to My Lou, I was back home at Plain View Farm!

· · · ·

PEARL'S WISDOM: WHEN the sun is gone and there is no light, as Papa told me, drop the reins and your trusty horses will surely find your way home.

Fishing with a Sack at Lake Norden

Dear Diary: I live with my family in South Dakota. It's a great place to live, but if you want to see anything new, you have to drive for miles.

One day, Papa wanted to use the car a neighbor offered us to enjoy, and he took us all out for a drive in the countryside.

Papa stopped the car that was carrying the family, at Lake Norden. We were by the bridge that stood where a stream was flowing from the lake.

I looked down and saw a lot of fish in the water. "I'd sure like to catch some fish!" I thought.

What was I to use? I didn't have a fishing pole, no line or hook, and of course no bait. But I went down to the water's edge, and then I saw a gunny sack on the ground.

"Why not a sack?" I thought.

Off with my socks and shoes, I went into the water. I stood and held the gunny sack open in the water, as cars crossed the bridge overhead.

The fish were travelling in groups, and a group of dozen or so bullheads and perch, swam right in! Soon, I had a sack full of fish!

I would have stood there and caught another sack full, but Papa couldn't wait for that.

We had to go with the one sack of fish I had caught.

The bullheads we scaled and threw in the pan to fry them. They were easy to eat, as they had few bones. But the perch!

The perch were a lot tastier than bullheads, but full of bones and hard to eat. They are not good for little kids, so Mama gave them to our neighbor. What fun that was, fishing for our dinner!

• • • •

PEARL'S WISDOM: WHEN you go fishing and don't have a fishing rod, use a gunny sack instead. You will be sure to catch a lot more fish in a lot less time!

Horses Can Do Amazing Things!

Dear Diary: One day I had to have the horse to help me get the cows out of the Slough. The water was up above their knees.

Papa wanted me to bring them home. But the cows loved the grass that grew above the water. I found I couldn't get them to move out of the Slough. All they wanted was to keep on grazing on that delicious, juicy grass.

What was I to do? I had to get them home!

The only thing I could think of was to command my horse, "Bite 'em!"

Well, guess what? My horse actually did bite the cows on their tails! And did they ever scramble to get out of that Slough then.

I still see it happening. Usually, though it was our dog Denver, who could really herd the cows.

Papa would command Denver to get the cows, and the dog would run and find the cattle. Sometimes over a mile away, he would round them up.

We had a lot of cattle then. Seven milking cows, and then the calves. Of course, there would be the bulls.

We also had a dog named Sandy, who was such a good dog. She could really dig up gophers in Mama's garden and out in our fields. But when it came to rounding up the cows, she wasn't all that good.

Thank goodness for Denver, and even my horse!

. . . . .

PEARL'S WISDOM: TO herd your cows, be sure that you have a horse who thinks he is a dog, or better yet a real dog named Denver.

Skunk in the Henhouse!

Dear Diary: Papa had a way to deal with skunks, that liked to burrow into the henhouse. The floor was all dirt, so they could easily get in that way.

Can you imagine the smell they would make? The chickens would be so upset, they wouldn't lay! He knew how to set traps for them. He would put a trap in the skunk's hole.

But one time he went to check the trap, to see if he had caught one. Yep, there was a skunk in the trap. But just then, it sprayed him right in the face, and even in his eyes.

He ran to the house, screaming for us to come out with a bucket of water. I ran out with a bucket of water, and he washed out his eyes, which were burning terribly.

We brought him a change of clothes, and then he went behind the shed and buried his skunky ones.

Later on, he would come and dig them up, so we could wash them. Burying them in dirt would take out the bad smell.

Another time, I encountered a skunk underneath the granary. We kids were playing Hide and Go Seek one night. When I looked, I saw two eyes of a skunk, peering right at me in the dark. I couldn't see the animal, just its eyes. I was scared it would spray me, just like it did my Papa. That was the end of Hide and Go Seek for me that night!

• • • •

PEARL'S WISDOM: IF you come across a skunk, make sure it is not backing up! Or else you will be in for a very smelly surprise!

Dear Diary: We took our baths each Saturday every week, to make a fresh start for the coming week.

Mama spent the whole day preparing the food, to provide meals for Sunday. She did not cook on Sunday in order to honor the Sabbath. Along with cooking on the wood stove, she heated water in the stove's reservoir.

The extra space on the stove top she used for heating pots of water.

When the day's main outdoor chores were done, we dragged out the big galvanized water tub from the basement. It was also used at times like a little pool in the backyard, when it grew so hot and muggy.

We found joyous relief in our little pool. The water was dragged up from the slough, in the stone boat drawn by horses. We called it the big trough, which Papa rigged up on skids, to help us clear the fields of stones.

Using a dipper, Mama poured in the hot water from the stove reservoir. She also poured in some of the water from the stone trough. Mama made sure that the water was cooled down sufficiently, so we could stand it.

She replaced the water in the reservoir to heat to bathe the baby, or the youngest child first before us big kids.

We helped Mama get water for this job. Whenever she needed water, we got it for her, so Mama didn't have to run back and forth, and back again.

The first and luckiest child got the most soap and cleanest water, plus Mama's vigorous scrubbing with lye soap.

Mama made the soap herself, using wood ashes and fat. She cooked them together over a fire, until it got solid enough to be poured into a pan. After it cooled it hardened. She then cut it into squares for use.

The lye soap worked for us, giving some suds. Mama, using a rag, scrubbed off our week-long build-up of grime. This came from working on the farm doing our chores.

Ouch! That deep-cleaning scrub hurt sometimes!

There were six of us girls, before any boys popped up in between our ranks. So, our hair had to be dealt with more gently, than a boy's.

Only rain water would do, as it was soft water. The ground water was so full of minerals, it stained the sinks red and made our hair, if washed in it, hard and stiff.

South Dakota our home state, wasn't the state that got a lot of rain, it was called the Sunshine State. We got more sun than moisture, and that meant we were a dry state. Although, snow came every winter to provide the needed wetness, to get our crops going.

After winter time, we had to pray and hope urgently for occasional thunderstorms. We needed this soft water for our crops, for baths and for washing our hair!

Into the tub each of us went in turn, going by age, youngest to oldest.

I was the eldest next to Papa, and he was last to get in the tub. As for Mama, I never knew what she did, as she had to take care of us. She saw to it that we all bathed sufficiently, to pass her inspection.

No gray areas behind our ears, our fingernails all clean, and a shine on our noses! I suspected all that scrubbing we got, which splashed so much water and soap on her, she considered that sufficient for her bath.

At last my time came to get in the tub. By this time, even with Mama's pouring in more heated water, the liquid in the tub was, alas, as thick as what we got out of the swampy slough in the south pasture!

Papa, dear Papa, had it worst, but he never complained. By the time he got into it, the water was mostly wet, lukewarm barely, and the suds were tired-looking, no sparkling bubbles by his turn.

We bundled up in towels, and dried our hair by the wood stove in the parlor. It was by this time, that Papa dared to dash into the kitchen, for his private bath.

When he took his first look at the tub and its contents, did he sigh and turn his eyes up and pray for endurance?

Papa never washed his hair. Why? He didn't want to stick his head in dirty washtub water! Instead he brushed it clean all his life. His hair was thick and he didn't lose it like so many men did. That brush did the trick for him!

Upstairs, as we prepared our hair for Sunday service, we were thankful whenever the rain water supply lasted enough for all of us. Sometimes we ran out. That left our hair hard to manage, if well water had to be added.

Imagine how that felt if you couldn't appear your best on Sunday!

• • • •

PEARL'S WISDOM: BATH day is a very good day, unless, you are the last kid or Papa! Then bath day for him, would be like a dip in the old slough!

Laundry Day on the Farm

Dear Diary: My brothers, sisters and I always took our baths on Saturday. This left Mondays to do all the necessary washing.

We washed our clothes, the tablecloths, towels, the bed sheets and pillow cases, Papa's work clothes, and whatever needed washing.

We girls had to help Mama as much as we could.

It was work, work, work for a family that grew to nine children. There were seven girls, two boys, and two adults of course, our beloved parents!

Monday was like any work day. We had to do our grubby chores in the barn and in the house, then helped out with the grubby laundry.

We didn't wear our nice clothes, when it was laundry day. Instead, we tied bandanas on our heads and wore our oldest clothes. What a sight our crew presented!

We hauled out the washtubs and scrubbing boards into the yard. In winter time, it was very difficult to wash clothes. It was very cold and of course, there was snow on the ground.

When it was summer time, it was too stifling hot. Which was easier to take? It was all hard work, hot or cold.

In this hot weather, we brought the tubs out. Mama heated the water in the kitchen, which only made the kitchen hotter.

We used a hand-cranked clothes washer, to turn and circulate the water, soap, and clothes. We girls took turns at that, and only we older ones could do it.

When Mama said it was time, we pulled out the clothes. We rinsed them in a tub of water, one piece at a time. Then we ran the item through the wringer with the wooden rollers, squeezing out the water.

On some clean boards, a pile of laundry grew. They were washed, rinsed, and wrung out clothing and other things. What an enormous pile!

Clothes' lines of rope, had to be strung up by Papa across the yard close to the house, which he did for us.

Would the wind cooperate, and not try to blow our clothes off the lines? In winter, the same wind froze our clothes stiff. They were stacked, until they thawed out in the kitchen!

How funny Papa's long-underwear looked standing on its own! I won't say how our girlish things looked, they made us giggle even more!

With a big bag of wooden clothes pins (many of which Papa carved), we were ready to attack the big pile.

The tallest of the girls, had to do the pinning of the clothes on the lines. Our little sisters had to stand on stools, and hoped that the wind wouldn't blow them off!

Mama helped us as much as she could. She was in the kitchen, getting a meal ready for us, for when we were finished with the laundry.

Imagine how we felt, hot, tired and perspiring. Mama would come out on the kitchen porch with a pot of coffee, cups and donuts. Each of us got a cup of coffee to savor, as coffee was a luxury on any day of the week! And not to mention, Mama's delicious donuts!

How adult and grown-up we all felt, sipping that brew, hot as we were. We knew we were needed and appreciated!

* * * *

PEARL'S WISDOM: LAUNDRY was hard work, winter and summer time, but special treats afterwards made it all worthwhile!

Papa and the Cup of Coins

Dear Diary: My Papa's name is Alfred Stadem and he is a very good farmer. He bought some land and added it to Plain View Farm. But before he bought it, he went and took a look at it first.

Did Denver the dog go along with him? Yes, I thought I heard him barking at a rabbit or a pheasant!

Well, the field had never been plowed before. It was a part of the vast, treeless Prairie, that covered these grassy, northeastern hills of the Dakotas, where the buffaloes and Indian tribes roamed.

One day, Papa had his horses out plowing the new field, when he noticed something in the furrow. He went to pick it up. It turned out to be an old cup.

"What was a cup doing here in the wide, open country?" he must have wondered.

More surprising to him, it held coins, and some of them were silver! He was holding someone's bank account in his hands! But who did this cup of coins belong to?

There were the Bands of Lakota Indians, who for ages, had hunted buffalos for their living. They had encamped on this piece of ground for a long time in the past.

Now the cup of coins was on Papa's land, and so the little treasure fell to him.

"Would they ever return for the cup of coins?" Papa thought.

Not likely. The cup was probably forgotten. The owner who knew its whereabouts, may have died years before Papa found it.

If only cups could tell stories, instead of just holding water, coffee, or orange juice! What would THIS cup say?

Why was it buried? Who buried it? How was the money earned? Where did the money come from? Was the money payment for a lot of pelts or buffalo hides?

We'll probably never know. The cup isn't telling its secrets! Whoever put the money there had passed on, perhaps forever, but still the money remained a Mystery in a cup.

· · · ·

PEARL'S WISDOM: AT the end of a well dug furrow, you may find a cup of silver coins!

How I Found a Bees' Swarm and Honey for the Family!

D ear Diary: One summer afternoon, I was coming from Bryant in the buggy, when I saw a swarm of bees beside the road in a ditch.

A thought came to me, "Wouldn't I like to see how we could make honey at the farm?"

I rushed home and told my Papa about it, and right away he was very interested. So, we drove back to where I saw the bees. He brought along a soft enough cloth, so they would stick to it.

He carefully put it over them, wrapped them in, and worked the cloth under them, then got them into the buggy. As we were riding home, Papa and I were talking.

"Pearl, what do you think we should put the bees in?" he asked. Then I had a brilliant idea. We had some discarded old junk in the yard. An old washing machine came to mind.

"I know Papa! Remember that old washing machine in the yard? That could work!" I said excitedly.

Papa went and found in the yard, back behind the trees, the discarded washing machine without even the wringer on it. It definitely could not be used anymore for washing clothes, but it sure would make a nice home for the bees.

Papa put them in the old washing machine, then covered them with a board. He put a small opening in it, so they could come and go. They liked it in there, and stayed.

We gave them molasses for food, to help them have something to eat in their new home. Soon they found trees on our farm to their liking. Some of the trees were cherry trees, which had plenty of blossoms they could get their food from.

We kept them in the winter too, and fed them more molasses.

Hooray! We had honey makers on the farm!

We loved to go and take honeycombs from the sides of the washer machine. Mama would put them on the back of the stove in a pan to melt slowly. She later poured off the honey into jars, then put them in the cool basement on shelves.

We usually kept all the can goods and honey below the built-out window, on the south side of the house.

That honey sure sweetened up the Stadem gang, which we surely needed with nine children living there!

. . . .

PEARL'S WISDOM: NEVER ever miss out on making your own honey, but first you will need some honey bees to do so. They will sure sweeten everything, even your day!

Honey Sweetens Up the Family!

Honey Sweetens Up the Family!

Papa's Gift of Agility

D ear Diary: Papa could jig up a storm and also do amazing things, which I have never seen anyone else do, especially at his age.

He would jig for us at home sometimes. The ground outdoors was not the best place for his special feat. He had to be on a level floor to do it.

One thing he could do was to jump over his folded hands, held in front of him. Us kids tried it and could never do it.

We all got a good laugh at our awkward attempts. I tried and tried, but couldn't copy Papa. How he learned to do that was beyond me. That was his special talent.

But Papa was a man of many talents, like water locating with a stick for many farmers around, well-digging, auctioneering, author, 4th of July band master, historian, landscaper and many other things.

Was there anyone else like our Papa? There couldn't be many people who could jump over their own handshake!

• • • •

PEARL'S WISDOM: JUMPING over your own handshake is not meant for everyone, only Papa!

Dear Diary: One day, I went with Bernice to visit Uncle Andrew and family at their home. It was a short walk to their farm just up the road toward Bryant.

When I offered to milk one of his cows, he said, "I have found some minnows in my well." I couldn't believe it.

He offered to show us. He dropped down a fish net scoop attached to a long rope. He drew it back up. In the scoop he pulled up three little fishes, no bigger than Bernice's finger.

I could hardly believe it!

"You can have them," he said, and he put the minnows in a coffee can with water.

We took them home and put them in Papa's pond at the back of the house. I had water lilies already growing in it, but no fish.

I didn't have any fish food, but Mama gave me some oat meal, so I threw them oatmeal. They loved it, and they grew large on that oatmeal!

Papa's pond was cement sided, dug out of the dirt. Whenever I went and looked at our pond, I could see it becoming more beautiful as time went by.

Not only was our pond looking beautiful with the little rock-edge and ferny brook flowing down, but the minnows now looking like large fishes, added to its beauty. I must not forget the real fountain in the center!

. . . .

PEARL'S WISDOM: PONDS certainly need fish. Ponds also need water lilies, a brook and even a fountain. They all make the pond so beautiful!

Dear Diary: Papa said farms need many things done every day to keep them working properly. You might have to put some oil in the tractor, or in the car so that they will keep working.

Fences are very important, especially for farms, if they are to do their job all week long, as they ought to. Livestock don't understand how important fences are to them. They need fences to keep them safely in, and keep unwanted animals out too.

Fences hold the livestock in, so they won't wander out on the road, and get run into by cars or trucks.

Fences also stop them from getting into the crops, and eating them all up. If you're fencing in chickens, geese and ducks, it's for their protection, so a fox or coyote won't get them.

Grazing animals like cows, horses, and sheep can even ruin the neighbor's corn. So, fences are very, very important to everybody in the community.

This is why a good farmer's duty is to walk along his fences, to see that they are doing their job.

If there is a hole in the fence, one of his animals might get out, or some wild animal might get in! Papa knew how important fences are on a farm, and he built them all himself.

But Papa also kept careful watch on them, and if they needed repairs, he did it on the spot.

What if he found a hole in his fence? He couldn't haul the fence in from the fields, to do the work in his workshop. No, he had to fix it where it was.

Sometimes, Papa didn't bring his wire cutters along. Was he going to leave that hole there, to come back later if he could? No! He knew he had to fix it right away, and besides, he had very strong teeth.

Papa's teeth must have been unusually strong, for he could actually cut through fence wire with them! Maybe there came a time that he found he had to stop using his teeth this way, because it was either hurting them, or they were chipping.

Papa's fences needed a lot of care. Livestock like cows and horses, love to rub their sides on the wire, to scratch an itch. Or they shove their heads through any place they can, just to get the greener grass outside the fence. You just can't watch them all the time, to stop them from doing those things. They are going to do them, being their nature.

In time, that makes a hole big enough for a whole animal to get through. No wonder Papa was always fixing his fences.

It wasn't exactly fun for Papa. It was real work, sometimes hard and sweaty work, with mosquitoes jabbing him or flies making a nuisance of themselves.

But it needed to be done, if the farm was to go right. Just as important, Papa wanted to keep his neighbors happy.

Any farmer who wasn't doing his job, would let his fences go. Soon his livestock was running everywhere, doing damage to others even themselves.

Papa was a neighbor-respecting farmer, and he wanted to make his farm go right. He also wanted to be as good a neighbor as he could be, and to do both, he had to keep his fences fixed.

· · · ·

PEARL'S WISDOM: MENDING fences is a must on a farm, but never ever use your teeth to cut the wire, like Papa. Wire cutters don't like it when their work is taken away!

Our Weekends at the Farm

Dear Diary: Have you ever wondered what weekends are like on a farm? Well, I don't know about other farms, but weekends on our farm is very special.

Our farm, called Plain View Farm, is a busy farm, except on Sundays.

We do the usual work during the week. Papa takes care of the big stuff and the hard work on the farm.

Mama takes care of the house, like winding up the clock every day, cooking and cleaning. She also takes care of us children too.

Me and my sisters and brothers, if they are old enough, have our chores to do too. We help Mama around the house, with the cleaning, or with the cooking. We also make sure that the dogs and cats are fed.

We also help Papa with feeding the chickens, the geese, and some of the livestock like the sheep or goats. The cows and horses are too big for us little kids to feed. Papa did that himself.

Mama make sure that we practice our musical instruments, or learn our hymns for choir at the coming Sunday Church service.

On Saturday, Mama especially spends most of her time on cooking three meals for Sunday. This way, she can devote herself to the Sabbath Day, without the distractions of meal preparations.

She "fenced in" Sunday to keep the Sabbath holy. Papa likewise "fenced in" Sunday in his way. He saw to it that he and the children got all the chores done to the point, where they wouldn't have to work on Sunday, like they did Monday through Saturday.

Once Sunday is over, then we are back to Monday, and back to our everyday chores.

· · · ·

***PEARL'S WISDOM: WORKING** seven days a week will make you dull; resting seven days a week will make you duller.*

How I Got Rid of Rats on The Farm

Dear Diary: One day, my father was going to shell corn we had picked. We had the corn stored in the barn at one end, and when he went to shell it, out came the rats.

You see, they were down underneath the corn, in holes they had made, and there they were, eating and eating.

So, when we got to the end of the shelling, and my dad was all through, the rats would come out one after the other from the ground there.

I don't know where I heard of it, or how I thought of it, but I had the most peculiar thought.

"I'm going to get some red paint and a brush and see if I can't catch 'em by opening the door part-ways. When they try to squeeze through and can't make it, I'd be right there to put my foot right on them and paint them."

I got some red paint and a brush, caught them in between the door and my foot and painted them red.

And in a day, they were all gone! There wasn't a rat in sight, because all the other rats were afraid, just scared to death. That's because the red rats chased them all off the farm, so we never had any rats after that!

· · · ·

PEARLS WISDOM: IF YOU can, always use red rats on your farm, they are great at keeping the other rats away!

Snapp! Crackles!
POPP!

Popcorn on the Cob!

Dear Diary: Papa needed me to weed the corn, as I was the oldest of the children. I went to the barn as he told me and got the hoe, which was taller than I was!

Oh, my! I felt the fierce heat of the day already in the morning. So, I tied my sun-bleached, once red checkered bandana on my head.

I began to swing the heavy hoe at the big weeds. The first swing was always the hardest. But as I continued to swing the hoe, chopping and uprooting the weeds, it got a little easier.

Despite my efforts, after a while I felt so hot and worn-out I had to stop. I knew I had to rest a bit before I continued.

As I stood leaning on my hoe, I looked up at the tall corn stalks above me. Toward the tops they were so ripe that the cornhusks had split open, and I saw corn kernels.

Now Papa always planted a row or two of popcorn every year. That way, we would have plenty of popcorn to pop for Christmas treats. We loved to string popcorn together. We put them on Mama's big fern we used for a Christmas tree in our parlor. After Christmas, we all ate the decorations!

We couldn't afford to decorate any more than that. No trees grew we could cut down, and buying a Christmas tree was out of the question for us.

I gazed up at the cobs above my head, and made a wish that came out as a prayer.

"Please make them pop. I would love to have some popcorn just now to chew on!"

I was just about to start back to work, when I heard a strange noise.

There was no wind, so the windmill wasn't turning. Nothing stirred in the baking hot sun.

I was going to swing the hoe against a big thistle, when—pop! I heard the sound again!

Then I heard a SNAP!

Down the row overhead something strange was happening.

Snap, crackles, pops! Snap, crackles, pops!

I had to see for myself if what I was hearing, was what I had prayed for.

With no ladders in the field, I had to figure out a way to get to the corn. Oh! I held a hoe.

By reaching up with the end of the hoe, I pulled the cob down low enough, so I could hop up to grab it.

I could not believe my eyes at first. Popcorn had popped on the cob, white and fluffy! My wishful prayer was answered!

In a flash it went into my mouth. I had the most delicious chew, before I set off to work with renewed purpose.

• • • •

PEARL'S WISDOM: BE careful making a prayer from a wish, while standing in the corn field on a hot day. You will be delightfully surprised and get popcorn!

Dear Diary: Mama and Papa had six girls and yet no boy! She felt bothered that neighbors might be talking about it.

Farms needed boys to do the rough, outdoor chores. Who besides Papa would plow the fields, plant them, weed them, and handle the stock?

Who? Us girls of course!

As soon as we all got old enough, we worked just as hard as boys! We had to do it, Papa had no one else, and he couldn't afford to hire a man.

Our excitement grew and grew, as we joined Mama in hoping for a boy each time, but it didn't happen. We didn't give up hoping though.

Mama said she prayed, "Oh, for the neighbors' sake, let it be a boy this time."

When it drew time for the baby to come, Mama told Papa to go get the doctor.

That was the first time she had ever wanted one to come to assist her. She said she felt it was going to be different this time, probably because the coming baby was bigger than we had been.

I will never forget the day. We were all at home, and Mama was feeling the baby was coming. The doctor arrived, and we waited outside the bedroom, practically holding our breath.

Caroline our dear aunt, was trained in nursing. She came to assist the doctor who came from town. Papa was around too, doing the chores, like keeping the stove hot to boil more water, and keeping the coffee pot going.

We were too many to hang around and be underfoot, so we had to stay clear of this undertaking.

Finally, there was a sound we all knew meant the baby had arrived!

We were thrilled! Was it a girl? Could it possibly be a boy, a baby brother?

Aunt Caroline called us, so we ran and crowded into the small bedroom on the ground floor, where Papa and Mama slept. Here the crib was set up beside the bed with a small passage between them.

The doctor stood up as we squeezed into the bedroom. We knelt down next to the bed, to see the baby Mama held in her arms.

"A boy, Mama?" I whispered to Mama, who lay against a pillow, worn out, her arms around the little bundle in her arms.

The baby's little red face screwed up and began to cry, and the doctor smiled.

"A boy," the doctor said. He patted my head.

Oh, the joy! Mama had the answer to her prayer, and we had a brand-new baby brother!

He was hoped for, and prayed for, for years, and now he is real, in Mama's arms!

My younger sisters urgently wanted to see the marvel, so I slipped back out into the kitchen, to give them a chance.

I went out the door on the north side that we used to get to the cellar. As I stepped out into the yard, I viewed the most amazing spectacle that I had never seen before or since.

For hours, rain had fallen and covered the trees, then frozen, and now presented a fairyland of ice crystals covering everything.

The trees looked like they were full of diamonds shining in the sun, from top to bottom! They stood out from the snow which was also covered in ice.

This very special day for us. We now have a baby brother, and Arthur was his name. I heard at school there was a famous king by that name in England. But we had someone even better in our own home by that same name!

· · · ·

PEARL'S WISDOM: BROTHERS are very special. So, if you hope hard enough and pray long enough, you just may get what you prayed for!

My Stubborn Horse!

Dear Diary: I was ready to start school last year, I was old enough. But Papa would not let me go to school alone, so he held me back one year. He wanted Bernice, my sister to go with me.

Bernice was not old enough last year, when I was ready to go to school. But she was ready this year.

Papa would bridle up the horse and put Bernice and me on it, and send us off to school.

This was a country school, two and a half miles away from the Farm. We went through the fields and didn't use the road.

Papa wouldn't let us use the road, as he was very cautious.

One morning, Bernice was sick and couldn't go to school with me.

So, Papa sent me along alone this time, but I didn't get very far. The horse, for some reason lay down on the ground.

Right away, I thought that the horse sensed something was wrong, because Bernice wasn't aboard.

I nudged him and nudged him with my heels, and still it wouldn't budge.

I knew if I got off, I wouldn't be able to get back on, not on that high horse.

We never had saddles in those days, so we rode bare back on the horses.

I didn't want to get to school late, so I finally got off the horse and began to walk.

As I got down the hill, I looked back, and saw that the horse had gotten up and started off for home.

I had a long, fast walk that day to get to school in time! The walk back home was just as long, if not longer!

. . . .

PEARL'S WISDOM: DONKEYS are stubborn animals, so I believe that my horse is really a donkey in disguise, and he fooled me, not to mention Papa! Always make sure that your horse is really a horse!

Horses Can Be Hazardous to Your Health!

Dear Diary: It was a nice, warm and sunny day. I was riding my horse home from school, when he went too close to a telephone pole. My shoe scraped against it, and made a noise that startled my horse, the silly creature!

All of a sudden, he reared up in the air, and I slid and fell onto my back on the ground. I hit the ground so hard, I saw stars.

I thought that I had broken my back. I lay there for a while, and then I got up.

I saw the horse had continued down over the hill. Then he stood there looking at me, his head held way up, as if he was thinking!

Just as soon as he saw that I was on my feet, he must have been satisfied that I was okay, because he turned away and started eating the grass. Silly creature!

. . . .

PEARL'S WISDOM: BEFORE you go anywhere on a horse, make sure he has ear plugs to block out any strange sounds!

Dear Diary: Mama cooked most of the day, especially on Saturday. Mama, Papa and our whole family, did all our work during the week. This was to make sure that we would be all prepared for being in Church on Sunday.

To help us with this goal, Mama worked harder than anyone else, I think. She rose up before Papa, to get the kitchen stove going. She used wood that had to be chopped. It had to fit in the part where it burned, to provide the heat. There was no electricity on our farm.

She could chop up an armful of wood outdoors so quick, and she was hard to beat!

We took our turns, once we were old enough to handle an ax right and not hurt ourselves. But Mama didn't wait for us. If she ran short in the kitchen wood bin, out she went and in a few minutes, she would return with the needed supply.

Mama used coals covered over by ashes from the last fire. She would start the fire that was going, to help her all day long. She used it for cooking the food, to feed us our breakfast, lunch, and dinner. She heated the water for our weekly scrub-down, in a big metal tub we set in the kitchen.

Once the bath was done, we were fed the last meal of the day. All the remaining food supply was put away for Sunday, when no meals were cooked.

We girls had our hair to attend to after our baths. We couldn't just go to bed, as our hair had to be dried and combed carefully. We tied a cloth over it to keep it in place, as we slept.

Our brothers would just hop in bed and pulled a sleep cap over their heads.

Girls' hair would look very strange if treated that way, all flattened down around our heads. No, we had to treat it a lot differently, or we would look a fright!

Mama, bless her heart, knew just how to end the day for us. She finished her last preparations in the kitchen and pantry, then went into the parlor to her beloved pump organ.

She put her tired feet upon the two places, where eventually worn places in the fabric appeared. Then we girls began to hear heavenly sounds from downstairs, come up the stairs to our bedrooms.

As we lay in bed, we listened to Mama singing and playing sacred songs.

Mama was not trained on the pump organ. She chorded it and did it very well too. As she sang, we listened. We felt the comfort her music gave us to prepare us for Sunday's worship, and fellowship with others in church.

When she was through singing and playing, we heard her at the foot of the stairs praying for us.

This was her routine she never once missed for our sake.

• • • •

PEARL'S WISDOM: MAMAS' are hard workers, maybe even harder than Papas', but they both love us just as hard!

?*#!$
Wash your
mouths!

How Papa Taught the Hunters a Lesson

Dear Diary: Mama's and Papa's little farm was good for growing corn. Papa knew how to grow it well too. Corn attracts pheasants, who love to pick up the stray kernels.

And after the big, plump pheasants, came the hunters.

Far off in the big city of New York, they heard all about the pheasants and how good the hunting was in the Dakotas.

A group of hunters came to Bryant, our home town, and they landed at Plain View Farm.

"May we hunt on your farm?" they asked Papa, when they showed up at the gate one day.

He said they could. But when they found no pheasants, they were upset, and some began to say bad words.

Papa spoke up. "There is to be no swearing on this land!" he told them. "We honor and respect each other and the Father's name here, and he shall not hold him guiltless who takes his name in vain!"

The hunters were surprised, but choosing not to be offended and angry, they listened to what Papa said.

Before long, they were blessed, for they shot their limit of pheasants. This made their trip a success.

The men returned to New York very happy. But they didn't forget their time on the little farm, out in the Dakotas. They met a respectable farmer.

They knew that Papa admired Abraham Lincoln. He was the president who defended the Union during the Civil War. He also freed the slaves. So, the hunters sent Papa a book about Abraham Lincoln.

In the end, I'm sure that Papa taught them a very valuable lesson that they will never forget!

• • • •

PEARL'S WISDOM: BAD words belong in the outhouse, and certainly not in anyone's mouth!

How Mama and I made ice-cream!

Dear Diary: I love ice cream! But we couldn't afford to buy ice cream in town. So, we had to make it ourselves.

We first had to have ice to start it. In the winter time I went down to the slough, and used a long handle stone mallet to smash up the ice.

I carried the chunks of ice in a gunny sack. Then Mama and I worked to make the ice cream.

We had plenty of cream, eggs, sugar, and salt. The salt was used to thicken the ice in the churn. It made the ice cold enough, to cause the mixed ice cream ingredients to freeze up. The sudden cold did the trick! It was like a miracle.

As soon as we had it made, we called everybody to have a bowl of it. It had to be eaten right then, as we had no freezer to keep it. Yummy homemade ice cream is so good. I love ice cream!

· · · ·

PEARL'S WISDOM: ICE cream is yummy, and better when it is home-made, and eaten right away!

How My Papa's Feet Saved the Day!

Dear Diary: Mama, Papa and my brothers and sisters, piled into the big, old sleigh, with lots of rugs and blankets. They kept us warm on a starry, cold and snowy Christmas Eve sleigh ride.

How excited we were! How we were looking forward to the Christmas decorations at church, and the special music of the choirs! We also had the Christmas story read from the Gospel of Luke in the Bible.

There were people singing joyous carols. But best of all, there were special bags of treats handed out to each child, at the end of the program.

All this took place beautifully, at a little church a few miles distant across the snowy hills.

Afterwards, on returning home, the sleigh, full of happy Stadem children, slipped too far over to the side of the road. It overturned into the ditch.

Uffdah! Everyone, including Mama holding the baby, was thrown out into the cold, deep snow. What a shock!

"Are you alright?" Papa called out to Mama and the baby.

"And you children, are you all okay?" Papa called out to us.

Then I heard Papa counting, as our heads appeared out of the snowy drifts.

"One, two, three…"

"We're all here Papa!" I said to him, as we tried to climb out of the snow, and back into the sleigh.

Our clothes and faces were covered with snow and ice. We weren't hurt, but it was an unpleasant experience.

Even worse than that, the gift bags of candy and fruits we all received, had landed in the snow. Where were they?

We anxiously looked, but not all could be found. It was so dark, and that made it impossible to see anything covered by the thick snow.

Now this was a terrible upset for us children! Christmas without this special bag of candy and fruits? What else could we get?

Maybe, this was all, since gift-giving was so expensive. It had to be kept to a minimum on Plain View Farm, which was a small farm for such a big family as ours to support.

Losing a bag of treats meant, one might go without any Christmas gifts that Christmas. How sad! We all counted on enjoying these precious gifts at Christmas.

Now what a sorry turn of events, it would seem on a day that was supposed to be full of joy and happiness! Try as they might, the children could not turn up all the bags!

Yet Papa was not the daddy to give in easily, where his family's happiness was concerned.

"...a few more missing," he said.

He thought carefully of what he could do to find them. He knew he couldn't see where the candy bags were hidden in the snow, but his feet could feel, couldn't they?

Sliding along, feeling carefully with his feet in the snow, he located the missing bags, and they were reunited with their happy owners.

Joy was restored to all hearts and faces, and the Stadem family sailed off toward home at Plain View Farm. Wow! At our Church in Bryant they gave us an orange and an apple, but no candy. Not any of us ever forgot that Christmas!

· · · ·

PEARL'S WISDOM: IF any time you lose your Goody bag in the snow, be sure to try Papa's technique! When it comes to snow, Papa proved feet can find things that eyes cannot see!

My mother Pearl Stadem, told me these stories and I just had to write them down. I did not want them to be forgotten, and besides, other people could enjoy them for a long time to come.

Mother told the stories almost every year at the reunions of the family on Plain View Farm, right up to age 100.

They were special stories that everyone loved to hear. As the years rolled on, more and more children got to hear them. The older ones heard them repeatedly, but that was okay, they still loved them the older they got.

Pearl Stadem told her stories under a tent, which was put up beside the house for her and the children to use. It was more fun to be there than in a shed.

What made Plain View Farm special is how much everyone loved it with all their heart, and continued to love it as long as they lived. Generations have sprung up and come to join together at reunions on the farm. Although most of the families' members were not born there, they still think of it as their own homeplace on the Prairie.

I am sure that you will think of it in the same way too, therefore, this is my warm welcome to you to come to Plain View Farm! Stay as long as you like! Kick off your shoes and make yourself comfortable when you get there. Have some donuts and something to drink! There will be plenty of hot coffee for the grownups. Lie on the grass. Sit back in the lawn chairs in the shade of the beautiful trees. Pick some old-fashioned, lavender or lilacs from the big hedges. They smell so fragrant. My mother Pearl helped Papa to plant and to care for them.

There will always be plenty fun for all, in the games you can play on the green, grassy acres. It is a safe place. The wide blue sky and rolling green hills of corn, make it a beautiful country. When you read Pearl's Diary, her stories will take you away on an imaginary visit to Plain View

Farm, but you can also pay us a visit time and again, since the gate is always left open for family and of course friends.

Bless you all,
Eben May

Thank you for reading The RetroStar Chronicles be sure to check out our other books in the series at our store below:

https://payhip.com/ButterflyProductions

Or check out our website at:

http://www.butterflyproductions838768487.wordpress.com

Or visit our Facebook page and leave us a comment. We look forward to hearing from you!

https://www.facebook.com/rdginther

Or you can write to us at:

rdginther42@yahoo.com

Don't miss out!

Visit the website below and you can sign up to receive emails whenever Eben May publishes a new book. There's no charge and no obligation.

https://books2read.com/r/B-A-YGIGB-IQRAD

Connecting independent readers to independent writers.

www.ingramcontent.com/pod-product-compliance
Lightning Source LLC
Chambersburg PA
CBHW021128130726
47988CB00003B/1212